JRJC

Cool Cake Mix Cupcakes

Fun & Easy Baking Recipes for Kids!

Alex Kuskowski

**Checkerboard
Library**

An Imprint of Abdo Publishing
www.abdopublishing.com

visit us at www.abdopublishing.com

Published by Abdo Publishing, a division of ABDO,
PO Box 398166, Minneapolis, Minnesota 55439. Copyright © 2015
by Abdo Consulting Group, Inc. International copyrights reserved
in all countries. No part of this book may be reproduced in any
form without written permission from the publisher. Checkerboard
Library™ is a trademark and logo of Abdo Publishing.

Printed in the United States of America, North Mankato, Minnesota
062014

092014

THIS BOOK CONTAINS
RECYCLED MATERIALS

Editor: Karen Latchana Kenney
Content Developer: Nancy Tuminelly
Cover and Interior Design and Production:
Colleen Dolphin, Mighty Media, Inc.
Food Production: Frankie Tuminelly
Photo Credits: Colleen Dolphin, Shutterstock

The following manufacturers/names appearing in this
book are trademarks: Betty Crocker SuperMoist®, Hershey's®,
Jell-O®, Land O Lakes®, Market Pantry®, McCormick®, PAM®,
Pillsbury Moist Supreme®, Proctor Silex®, Roundy's®

Library of Congress Cataloging-in-Publication Data
Kuskowski, Alex, author.
  Cool cake mix cupcakes: fun & easy baking recipes for kids! /
Alex Kuskowski.
     pages cm. -- (Cool cupcakes & muffins)
  Audience: 8-12.
  Includes index.
  ISBN 978-1-62403-299-8
1. Cupcakes--Juvenile literature. 2. Cake--Juvenile literature. I.
Title.
  TX771.K86 2015
  641.8'653--dc23
                    2013043079

To Adult Helpers

Assist a budding chef by
helping your child learn to cook.
Children develop new skills, gain
confidence, and make delicious
food when they cook. Some recipes
may be more difficult than others.
Offer help and guidance to your
child when needed. Encourage
creativity with recipes. Creative
cooking encourages children to
think like real chefs.

Before getting started, have ground
rules for using the kitchen, cooking
tools, and ingredients. There
should always be adult supervision
when a sharp tool, oven, or stove is
used. Be aware of the key symbols
described on page 9. They alert
you when certain things should be
monitored.

Put on your apron. Taste their
creations. Cheer on your new chef!

Contents

For the **Love** of Cupcakes!   4

The Basics   6

Cool Cooking Terms   8

Symbols   9

Frosting Tips   10

Kitchen Supplies   12

Ingredients   14

Red Delicious Cupcakes   16

Double Chocolate Dream   18

Best Cake Batter Cakes   20

Vanilla Orange Pop-ups   22

Sweet Angel Food Bites   24

Carrot Supreme Cupcakes   26

Mini Cheesecake Cookies   28

Conclusion   30

Web Sites   30

Glossary   31

Index   32

For the Love of Cupcakes!

Discover the wide world of cupcakes. Cupcakes come in every size, shape, and color. Cupcakes are fun to make and eat!

Use cake mixes to make quick cupcakes. Once they're done you can frost them any way you like. Your friends will be amazed at your cupcake creations. Try each of the recipes in this book. Or get creative and make up your own!

This book has everything you need to get started. It's filled with fun recipes. Follow each recipe's easy steps to create tasty treats. Get inspired to create cupcakes that taste and look great!

The Basics

Ask Permission

Before you cook, ask **permission** to use the kitchen, cooking tools, and ingredients. If you'd like to do something yourself, say so! Just remember to be safe. If you would like help, ask for it! Always ask when you are using a stove or oven.

Be Prepared

→ Be organized. Knowing where everything is makes cooking safer and more fun!

→ Read the directions all the way through before starting the recipe. Remember to follow the directions in order.

→ The most important ingredient is preparation! Make sure you have everything you'll need.

Be Neat and Clean

→ Start with clean hands, clean tools, and a clean work surface.

→ Tie back long hair to keep it out of the food.

→ Wear comfortable clothing and roll up your sleeves.

→ Put on an apron if you have one. It'll keep your clothes clean.

Measuring

Many ingredients are measured by the cup, tablespoon, or teaspoon. Measuring tools may come in many sizes, but the amount they measure should be printed or **etched** on the sides of the tools. When measuring 1 cup, use the measuring cup marked 1 cup and fill it to the top.

Some ingredients are measured by weight in ounces or pounds. The weight is printed on the package label.

Be Smart, Be Safe

→ Never cook if you are home alone.

→ Always have an adult nearby for hot jobs, such as ones that use the oven or the stove.

→ Have an adult around when using a sharp tool, such as a knife or a **grater**. Always be careful when using these tools!

→ Remember to turn pot handles toward the back of the stove. That way you avoid accidentally knocking the pots over.

No Germs Allowed!

Raw eggs and raw meat have bacteria in them. These bacteria are killed when the food is cooked. But bacteria can survive on things the food touched and that can make you sick! After you handle raw eggs or meat, wash your hands, tools, and work surfaces with soap and water. Keep everything clean!

Cool Cooking Terms

Here are some basic cooking terms and actions that go with them. Whenever you need a reminder, just turn back to these pages.

Wash

Always wash fruits and vegetables well. Rinse them under cold water. Pat them dry with a **towel**. Then they won't slip when you cut them.

Mix

Mix means to stir ingredients together, usually with a large spoon or electric mixer.

Whisk

Whisk means to beat quickly by hand with a whisk or a fork.

Symbols

Hot!

This recipe requires the use of a stove or oven. You will need adult **supervision** and assistance.

Sharp!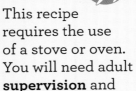

This recipe includes the use of a sharp **utensil** such as a knife or **grater**. Ask an adult to help out.

Frosting Tips

Learn the basics of frosting fun!

With frosting, the possibilities are endless. You can make frosting any color and shape you want. Check out these tips to become a master chef!

Frosting the cupcake

1. Fill a plastic bag with frosting. Press out the extra air. Seal the bag closed.

2. Pinch one corner of the bag flat. Cut off the corner. You can cut it straight across, or in a V shape or M shape. This is the bag's tip.

3. Hold the bag with the tip pointed down.

4. Squeeze the bag to push out the frosting. Start on the outside edge of the cupcake. Go around the edge.

5. When you reach the beginning of the circle keep going. Make smaller and smaller circles. This creates a **spiral**.

6. Stop squeezing when finished.

V shape

M shape

straight
across

Kitchen Supplies

measuring cups

mini muffin tin

mixing bowls

measuring spoons

scoop

spatula

electric mixer

muffin tin

paper liners

plastic bags

whisk

13

Ingredients

Here are some of the ingredients you will need:

chocolate
cake mix

carrot
cake mix

angel food
cake mix

no-bake
cheesecake mix

white
cake mix

German chocolate
cake mix

food
coloring

yellow sprinkle
cake mix

semi-sweet
chocolate
chips

chocolate
sandwich
cookies

orange gelatin

unsweetened
cocoa powder

multicolored
sprinkles

chocolate
sprinkles

vanilla
pudding mix

vegetable
oil

orange
extract

heavy whipping
cream

vanilla
extract

Red Delicious Cupcakes

Ingredients

CUPCAKES
1 18.5-oz. German chocolate
    cake mix
½ cup unsalted butter, softened
1 cup buttermilk
½ cup water
½ cup vegetable oil
2 eggs
1 tablespoon unsweetened
    cocoa powder
10 drops red food coloring

FROSTING
½ cup unsalted butter, softened
1 8-oz. package cream cheese
2 cups powdered sugar
1 teaspoon vanilla extract

Tools

paper liners
2 muffin tins
mixing bowls
electric mixer

measuring cups & spoons
scoop
spatula
plastic bag

1   **Preheat** the oven to 350 degrees. Put paper
    liners in the muffin tins.

2   Put all of the cupcake ingredients in a large
    mixing bowl. Beat with an electric mixer.

3   Divide the batter evenly between the
    muffin cups. Bake and cool as directed
    on the cake mix box.

4   Make the frosting. Put the butter and cream
    cheese in a medium bowl. Beat with an
    electric mixer until creamy. Mix in the
    powdered sugar and vanilla extract.

5   Remove the cupcakes from the muffin tins.
    Frost the cupcakes as shown on pages 10 and 11.

Double Chocolate Dream

MAKES 24 SERVINGS

Ingredients

CUPCAKES
1 18-oz. chocolate cake mix
1 cup mayonnaise
1 cup water
3 eggs

FROSTING
2 cups unsalted butter, softened
5 cups powdered sugar
2 teaspoons vanilla extract
½ cup semi-sweet chocolate
    chips, melted
chocolate sprinkles

Tools

paper liners
2 muffin tins
mixing bowls
measuring cups & spoons
spatula

electric mixer
scoop
dinner knife
small bowl

1   **Preheat** the oven to 350 degrees. Put paper liners in the muffin tins.

2   Put all of the cupcake ingredients in a large mixing bowl. Beat with an electric mixer.

3   Divide the batter evenly between the muffin cups. Bake and cool as directed on the cake mix box.

4   Make the frosting. Put the butter, sugar, vanilla extract, and melted chocolate in a medium bowl. Beat with an electric mixer until creamy.

5   Remove the cupcakes from the muffin tins. Use a knife to frost the cupcakes. Roll the tops of the cupcakes in the sprinkles.

Best
Cake Batter
Cakes

MAKES 24 SERVINGS

Ingredients

CUPCAKES
1 18-oz. yellow sprinkle cake mix
⅓ cup vegetable oil
1 cup buttermilk
4 eggs
1 teaspoon vanilla extract
¼ cup multicolored sprinkles

FROSTING
½ cup unsalted butter, softened
2 cups powdered sugar
½ cup yellow sprinkle cake mix
1 teaspoon vanilla extract
1 tablespoon whole milk
¼ cup multicolored sprinkles

Tools

paper liners
2 muffin tins
mixing bowls
whisk
measuring cups & spoons

scoop
electric mixer
spatula
plastic bag

1 **Preheat** the oven to 350 degrees. Put paper liners in the muffin tins.

2 In a large mixing bowl, whisk together the cake mix, oil, buttermilk, eggs, and vanilla extract. Add the sprinkles. Stir lightly.

3 Divide the batter evenly between the muffin cups. Bake and cool as directed on the cake mix box.

4 Make the frosting. Put the butter and sugar in a medium bowl. Beat with an electric mixer until creamy. Mix in the cake mix, vanilla extract, and milk.

5 Remove the cupcakes from the muffin tins. Frost the cupcakes as shown on pages 10 and 11. Sprinkle multicolored sprinkles on top.

Vanilla Orange Pop-ups

MAKES 62 SERVINGS

Ingredients

CUPCAKES
1 18-oz. white cake mix
1 package vanilla pudding mix
1 package orange gelatin
1¼ cups orange juice
⅓ cup vegetable oil
4 eggs
1 teaspoon vanilla extract

FROSTING
1 cup unsalted butter, softened
6 cups powdered sugar
¼ cup orange juice
1 teaspoon vanilla extract
¼ teaspoon orange extract
2 to 3 drops of orange food
     coloring

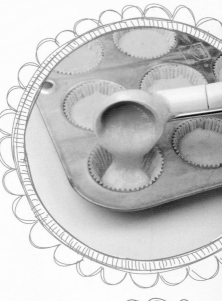

Tools

paper liners
mini muffin tins
mixing bowls
whisk

measuring cups & spoons
scoop
plastic bag

1 **Preheat** the oven to 350 degrees. Put paper liners in the muffin tins.

2 In a large mixing bowl, whisk together all of the cupcake ingredients.

3 Divide the batter evenly between the muffin cups. Bake 8 minutes. Cool as directed on the cake mix box.

4 Make the frosting. Put the butter and sugar in a medium bowl. Beat with an electric mixer until creamy. Mix in the juice, vanilla extract, orange extract, and food coloring.

5 Remove the cupcakes from the muffin tins. Frost the cupcakes as shown on pages 10 and 11.

Sweet Angel Food Bites

MAKES 62 SERVINGS

Ingredients

CUPCAKES
1 16-oz. angel food cake mix

FROSTING
1 pint heavy whipping cream
2 tablespoons white sugar
1 teaspoon vanilla extract
red and blue food coloring

Tools

paper liners
mini muffin tins
mixing bowls
electric mixer

measuring cups & spoons
scoop
spatula
plastic bag

1   **Preheat** the oven to 350 degrees. Put paper liners in the muffin tins.

2   Put the cake mix and 1¼ cups water in a large mixing bowl. Beat with an electric mixer.

3   Fill the muffin cups three-fourths full of batter. Bake 8 minutes. Cool as directed on the cake mix box.

4   Make the frosting. Put the heavy whipping cream, sugar, and vanilla extract in a medium bowl. Beat with an electric mixer until creamy. Mix in 3 drops each of red and blue food coloring.

5   Remove the cupcakes from the muffin tins. Frost the cupcakes as shown on pages 10 and 11.

Carrot Supreme Cupcakes

MAKES 24 SERVINGS

Ingredients

CUPCAKES
1 18-oz. carrot cake mix
1 cup buttermilk
½ cup vegetable oil
4 eggs
½ teaspoon nutmeg
½ teaspoon cinnamon

FROSTING
½ cup unsalted butter, softened
1 8-oz. package cream cheese
2 cups powdered sugar
1 teaspoon vanilla extract

Tools

paper liners
2 muffin tins
mixing bowls
whisk
measuring cups & spoons

scoop
electric mixer
spatula
plastic bag

1   **Preheat** the oven to 350 degrees. Put paper liners in the muffin tins.

2   Put all of the cupcake ingredients in a large mixing bowl. Beat with an electric mixer.

3   Fill the muffin cups two-thirds full of batter. Bake and cool as directed on the cake mix box.

4   Make the frosting. Put the butter and cream cheese in a medium bowl. Beat with an electric mixer until creamy. Mix in the powdered sugar and vanilla extract.

5   Remove the cupcakes from the muffin tins. Frost the cupcakes as shown on pages 10 and 11.

Mini Cheesecake Cookies

MAKES 12 SERVINGS

Ingredients

1½ cups graham crackers, crushed

¼ cup brown sugar

7 tablespoons unsalted butter, softened

1 11.1-oz. package no-bake cheesecake mix

1½ cups whole milk

¾ cup chocolate sandwich cookies, crushed

Tools

paper liners

muffin tin

whisk

measuring cups & spoons

mixing bowls

electric mixer

scoop

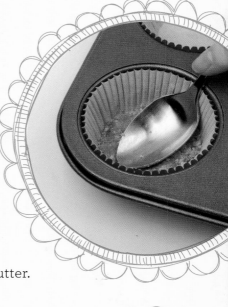

1   Put paper liners in the muffin tin.

2   In a large mixing bowl, whisk together the crushed graham crackers, brown sugar, and butter.

3   Divide the graham cracker mixture evenly between the muffin cups. Press it flat with the back of a spoon.

4   Put the cheesecake mix, milk, and crushed cookies in a large bowl. Beat with an electric mixer.

5   Divide the cheesecake mixture evenly between the muffin cups. Freeze 1 hour.

Tip: Crush more chocolate cookies. Use them to decorate the tops of the cupcakes before you freeze them!

Conclusion

Cake mix cupcakes can taste great! Making cupcakes that look amazing doesn't have to be hard. It can be easy and fun!

This book has tons of fun recipes to get you started. There's more to discover, too. Check your local library for more cookbooks on cupcakes. Or use your imagination and whip up your very own creations!

You can make cupcakes for birthdays, holidays, or just for fun. Your friends and family will love tasting your sweet creations. Become a muffin tin chef today.

. . . .

Web Sites

To learn more about cool cooking, visit ABDO online at www.abdopublishing.com. Web sites about cool cooking are featured on our Book Links page. These links are monitored and updated to provide the most current information available.

Glossary

etch – to carve into something.

grater – a tool with rough-edged holes used to shred something into small pieces.

permission – when a person in charge says it's okay to do something.

preheat – to heat an oven to a certain temperature before putting in the food.

spiral – a pattern that winds in a circle.

supervision – the act of watching over or directing others.

towel – a cloth or paper used for cleaning or drying.

utensil – a tool used to prepare or eat food.

Index

A

adult helpers, guidelines for, 2

angel food cupcakes, recipe for, 24–25

B

bacteria, in raw eggs and meat, 7

C

carrot cupcakes, recipe for, 26–27

cheesecake cupcakes, recipe for, 28–29

chocolate cupcakes, recipe for, 18–19

cleanliness, guidelines for, 6, 7

cooking terms, 8

creativity, in cooking, 2, 4, 30

F

frosting, guidelines for, 10

I

ingredients
measuring of, 7
preparing of, 6
types of, 14–15

K

kitchen supplies, 12–13

kitchen use
permission for, 6
rules for, 2

M

measuring, tools for, 7

O

orange cupcakes, recipe for, 22–23

P

preparation, for cooking, 6

R

recipes, reading and following, 4, 6, 9

red delicious cupcakes, recipe for, 16–17

resources, about making cupcakes, 30

S

safety, guidelines for, 2, 6, 7, 9

symbols, with recipes, 9

V

vanilla–orange cupcakes, recipe for, 22–23

variety, in cupcakes and frosting, 4, 10

W

Web sites, about cooking, 30

Y

yellow cupcakes, recipe for, 20–21